CHRISTMAS
MEDLEYS & VARIATIONS

Favorite Christmas Music Arranged in 3 Medleys and 2 Sets of Variations for Intermediate Pianists

Catherine Rollin

There is no better way to celebrate the holiday season than with the gift of music. Familiar Christmas carols and other holiday songs are sources of joy to many during this happy time of the year. It has been a great pleasure for me to explore the many facets of these beautiful traditional melodies and transform them into medleys and variations. I hope students and teachers will experience this same pleasure when playing them.

Merry Christmas!

Catherine Rollin

Copyright © MMII by Alfred Publishing Co., Inc.
All rights reserved.   Printed in USA.
ISBN 0-7390-2890-1
Cover art courtesy of PhotoDisc and Artville

A Jolly and Jingly Christmas Medley

Arr. by Catherine Rollin

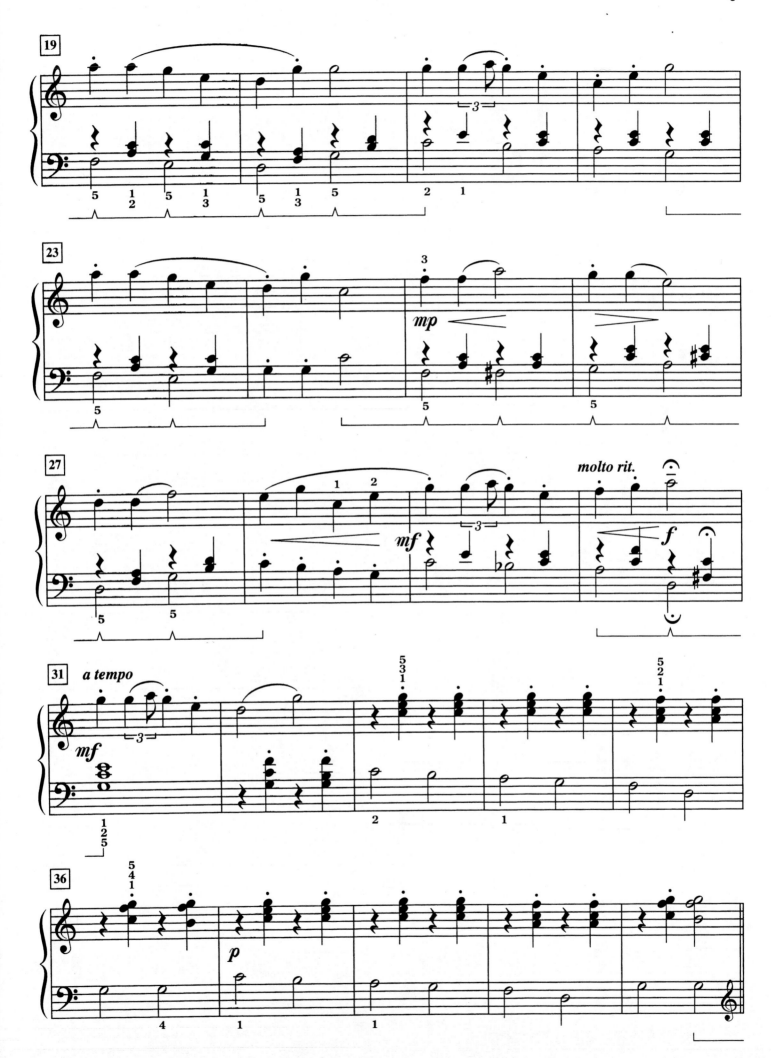

"Jolly Old Saint Nicholas"

"Jingle Bells"

LH legato

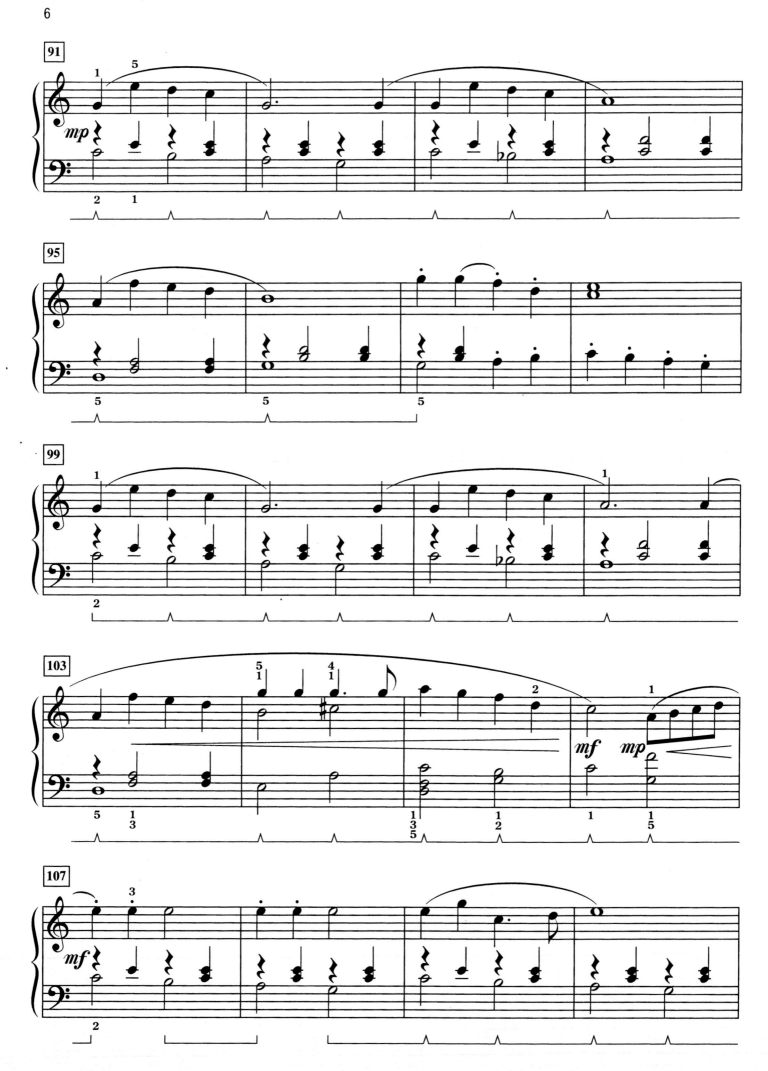

Hallelujah Medley

Arr. by Catherine Rollin

Tempo I

"Joy to the World"

Moderato
"Hark! The Herald Angels Sing"

God Rest Ye Merry Medley

Arr. by Catherine Rollin

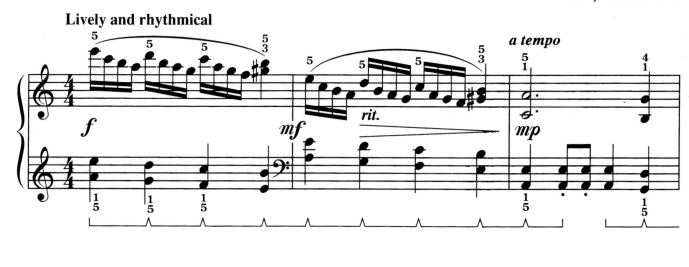

"God Rest Ye Merry, Gentleman"

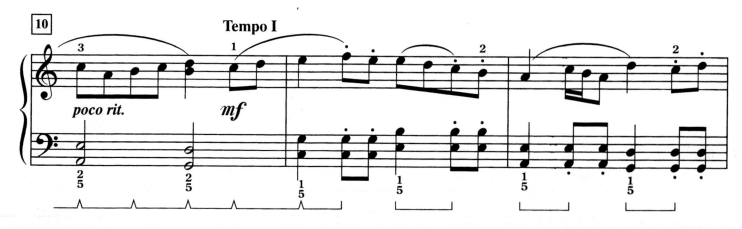

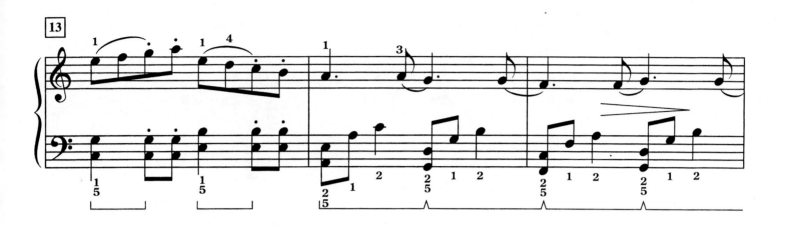

Slightly slower than Tempo I
"We Three Kings of Orient Are"

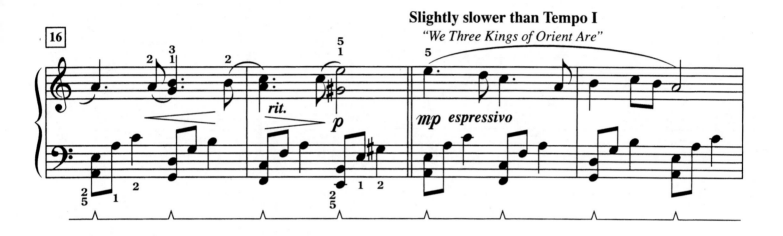

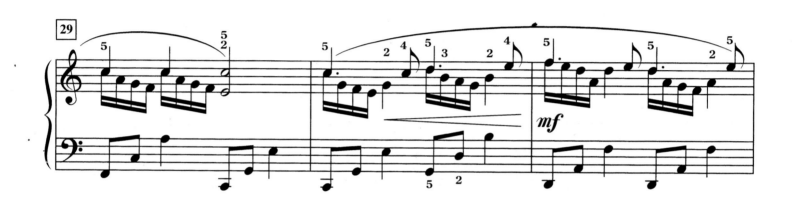

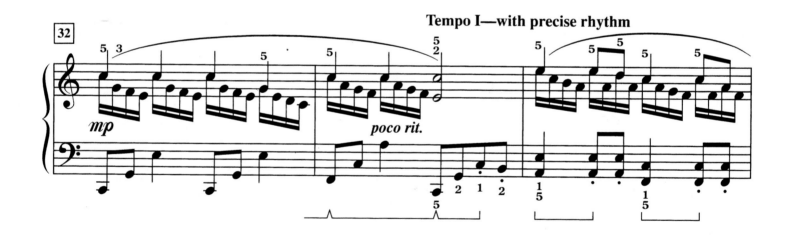

Tempo I—with precise rhythm

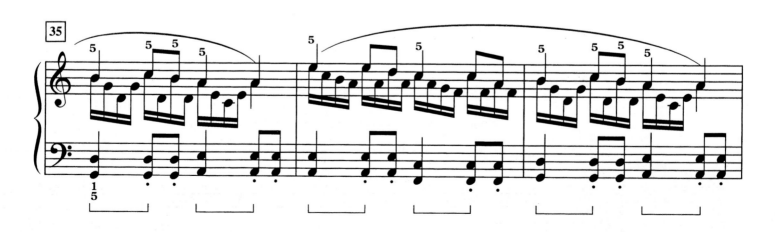

"What Child Is This?"

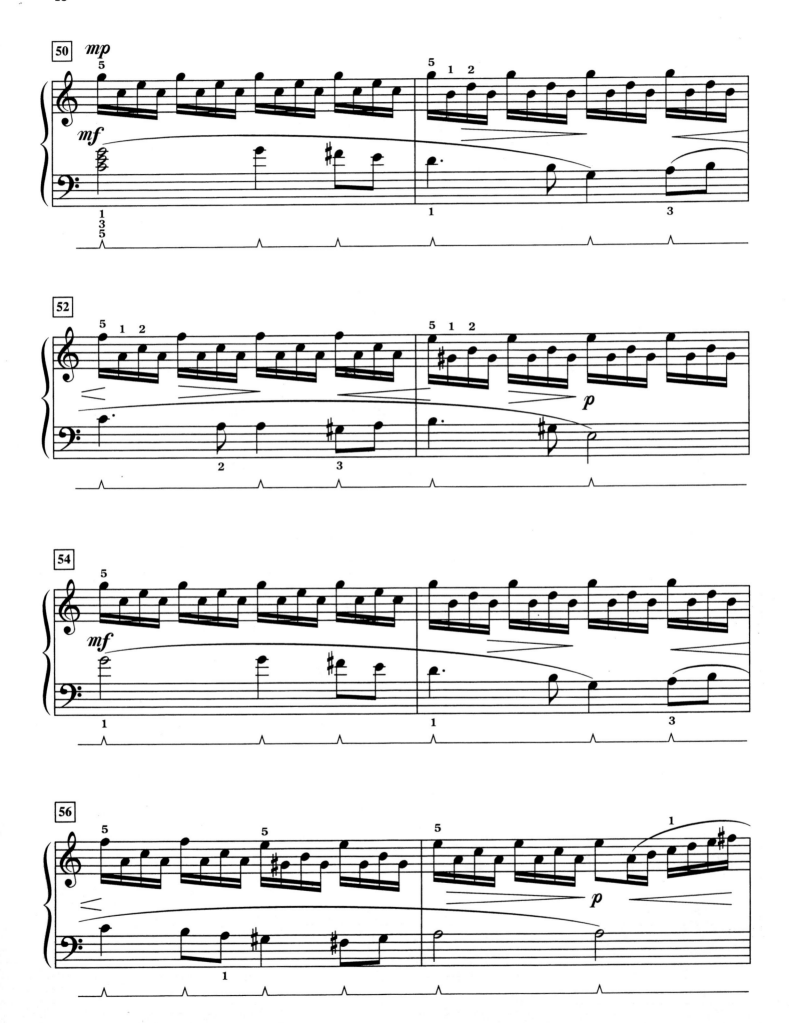

Variations on
We Wish You a Merry Christmas

Traditional
Arr. by Catherine Rollin

Variation I　25

Cheerfully and precisely

Variations on
O Christmas Tree

Traditional
Arr. by Catherine Rollin

Moderately, with sweet simplicity

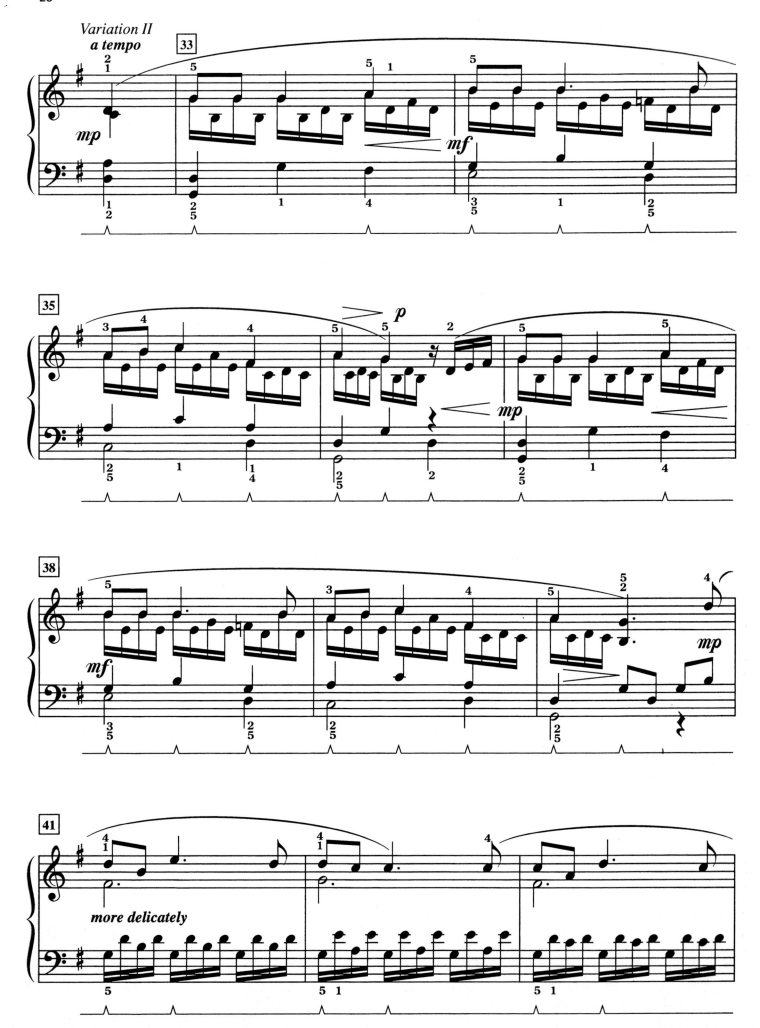

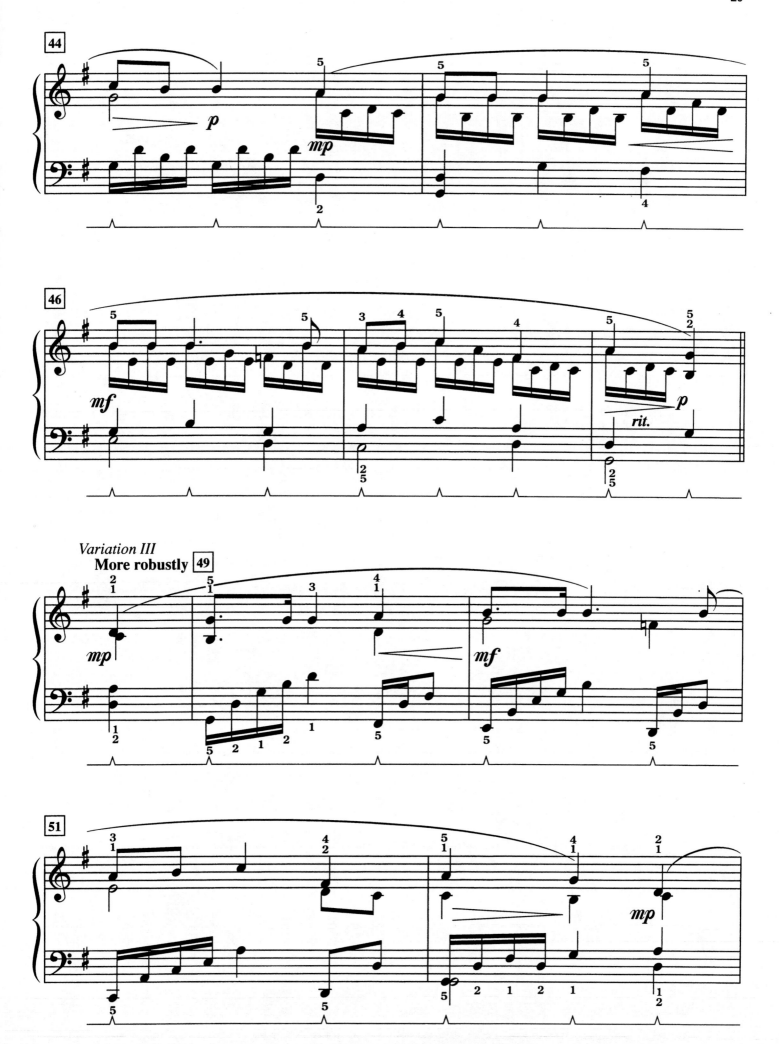

Variation III
More robustly 49